DREAMING
IN
PURPLE

L U N A I R I S

*My prismatic reality of
life, love, loss
motherhood
and magic*

For more writing by *LUNAIRIS,*
follow @lunairispoetry on Instagram.

ISBN: 978-1-9994921-0-6

DREAMING
IN
PURPLE

sunsets shared with you
exist only in my dreams
soon our sun will rise

for
every woman
every mother
every daughter
every goddess
who has been set on fire
and survived
with flying colors

for you

Contents

A LETTER TO MY DAUGHTER
THE IMPORTANCE OF WORDS
SPECIAL THANKS
ABOUT THE WRITER
IN LOVING MEMORY

WHEN RED MEETS BLUE

something magical happens
when two souls meet again
not quite love at first sight
love was created by the universe
it always existed
but instant recognition
a spark
of remembrance
from another lifetime
in a single colossal moment
time around you will freeze
the walls you built will crumble
every foundation of your being will quake
all of your senses merge at once
the entire world oblivious
to what just happened
between the two
when your eyes meet theirs
they feel what you feel
you will know
when red
meets blue

- a spark of purple

Messages

i*F* you are to hold
my words *I*n your hands
caress them ge*N*tly
keep them safe as you can
find my love within your min*D*
read between the lines
as you would a fragile soul
this is the drea*M*
that is min*E*

- if you can.

PURPLE

I want to know
how red and blue
make purple

for they trust in each other
an equal balance

not too much and
not too little
it can easily turn bad

just the perfect amount of each
can make a color so lovely

even a rainbow
could not live
without it

WISHING STARS

sometimes I can't trust the stars
and it breaks my heart to say that
because I have always been
in awe of their beauty
as if the hope inside me
forever wished
that they could light up my life
when I looked at them
the way stars light up a pitch-black sky
dancing and shining so bright
you don't even notice
the empty spaces around them

I was jealous
of how they made
every dark corner sparkle
but not mine

sometimes I can't trust the stars
so I wish upon them twice
because the first wishes
never came true

BELLY OF THE BEAST

all the monsters that set me free
let me live, let me breathe
built my strength on falling knees

what I thought was a gracious favor
was tenfold worse, I dread to savour

threw me into the belly of the beast instead
inescapable claws, flames of red

one that claimed love with abysmal eyes
suffocating shadows, demons in disguise

tightened his chains around me as I fell
this monster would not let me escape
his hell

MISSING

all I will miss
is the way the sun
so beautifully
kissed the mountains
good morning
and
good night

GRAVE ROBBER

do not unearth
the graveyard of my past
while I am planting flowers
transforming myself
into a garden

- let it rest, the future is growing.

I Am The Universe

I am
so much more than space dust
made by the universe
eyes of cosmic design
breathing galaxies into my lungs
shooting starlight
through my veins

I am
stronger than a supernova
as powerful as the sun
no, *every sun*
that ever existed
and then some

I am
worth every constellation
every star in the sky
even those that collapsed
in on themselves
and burned

I am the universe

I am alive

FALLING STARS

I still decorate, arranging stars
in my own expanding night sky
thousands for
every smile, every love
every tear, every loss
until it sparkled bright enough
to be seen with closed eyes
and oh god did they glisten
as I danced free beneath them
in awe of a lifetime of magic
yet stars are still falling
to illuminate my heart
as beautiful
as it is tragic

GRAVITY OF US

you pull me like the tides
when I try to push away
a force of nature truly
one I can't escape
for you are always with me
that I cannot deny
a transcendental calling
that draws me back alive
and I do return an instant
though I always fear it too
a power that's between us
the gravity
of me and you

REBIRTH

everything blooms

everything dies

everything grows

again

HER WALL

is flames burning
hotter than hellfire
prepared to burn anyone
who attempts to touch her
with sinful hands

is lightning
ready to strike down
in the path of the one
who dares to step too close to her
bearing deceit

is a raging tsunami
a torrent waiting to be unleashed
that will drown and destroy
everything around it
so that she can remain intact

is a howling vortex
aching to consume and remove
those who intend to betray her

and behind her wall, she is safe
she is invincible

Story

my life
is a storybook
a tragedy
an epic

it is not a
fairytale
or happily ever after

with many pages hidden
from all but me
that will reveal
why I am
who I am

you've only read a few words
but I am a novel
and darling
I've locked away those chapters
forever

CHANGES

before I held you
I wasted time
I hated myself
I was careless
I was reckless
I was lost
I felt like giving up

when I held you
I found my future
I found my reason
to fight
to be strong
to breathe
to live
to love

and my life was worth living for you

- to my daughter.
- thank you for saving me.

The Last Night

you never know when
it's the last time to tuck them in
sing them to sleep, hold little hands
mama don't rush these moments

these nights too
will grow old as they do
hold them closer a little longer
a little tighter, a little stronger

cherish each goodnight kiss
arms wrapped in comforting bliss
little smiles as their dreams take flight
mama, hold them close
until the last night

MISSING PIECES

why do you tear me apart
and crack me open
searching frantically for something
anything but me
what are you looking for
you will only find
missing pieces
of yourself
in here

oh

now I understand

ANGEL WINGS

I carried you in me
for only a short while
before you grew
your angel wings
you wanted to be
free and happy
somewhere else
somewhere beautiful
in a less cruel world
destined for a higher purpose
and I will always carry you
in my heart
and in my soul
until we meet again

FIREWORKS

as my eyes closed shut
a final tear fell from them
and all I dreamt of
were fireworks
flashing, exploding
and screaming
in my head

GALAXIES

you have galaxies
in your eyes
a universe expanding
over a lifetime
and every star glistens
with a secret
a wonder
a mystery
how lucky I am
to be one of them

USE YOUR VOICE

if you ever tell a man "no"
when he pursues you
and he proceeds to
do it anyway, belittle you
attack you, force you, push you
blame you, destroy you
or all of the above

darling, you need to run
and never look back

you are worth so much more
than someone's poisonous
excuse for love

you deserve so much more
than to be drowned
by someone else's darkness

- note to self.

CONTROL

I am not yours
you do not own me
I am not
chained to you, bound to you

you cannot drag me back
when I run away
when I break free
from your darkness

you will not tighten
your shackles, your noose
around me ever again

I am *mine*

I am *free*

you have no control over me
anymore

My Joy

the purest love is your child's arms
wrapped around you
their smile the reason for yours
the hope and wonder and love
in their eyes as they look at you

it's the comfort of a hug
after a long day
and drying every tear, happy or sad
it's sharing every laugh, every cry
never leaving their side
guiding them gently through life

it's waking up to the sweetest kisses
and every "I love you mommy"
that makes every day worth living

the purest of loves, perhaps
is the love between a mother
and her child

WANDERING

if you ever feel lost
go where your feet and heart
carry you

believe in yourself
trust in yourself
and you will find yourself
exactly where you need to be

MY SUNSHINE

when you were born
the sun shone so bright
inside and all around me

you brought light into my life
and I was warm again

you are my sunshine
my guiding light
my beacon of hope

my love for you
is a roaring flame
that will never, ever
burn out

even when the skies
are grey

- I love you to the moon and beyond.

REBORN

life is a string of continuous end
every bead added a new form
plucked gently
by the hands of the universe
karma's thread is never torn

she knows precisely
which beads to choose
some sparkle eternally
blacken, tarnish

it all depends on
you dear soul
the life you live, if honest

if you are lucky and you are reborn
into a blinding, luminous bead of life

ensure the next is just as large
brimming
with endless light

NEW MOON

she lived her life
like the phases of the moon
a crescent of light to become
so much fuller

to fulfill her hopes and dreams
to build her strength and potential
in all of her wondrous entirety

as the days and nights
move through time
as she turned the tides
and arose many storms
only to calm them herself
with grace and beauty
before settling into the horizon

to begin her next phase
to live her life again
as new

LEAVING

leave your troubles behind
and as the sun sets
this chapter ends
fly towards a new beginning
a new life
as the sun rises
with you

Slow Dancing

tonight
I am slow dancing
on my own
my body and hips
sway to silent rhythm
closed memory-filled eyes
arms embracing my waist
starlit fingers grasping
red hair out of place
carefree for a moment
a bittersweet world
remembering
when I was a little girl

I smile and twirl fast
laugh until tears cascade
falling down as I do
I make a wish that won't fade
a wish on this moment
to last for me
woman, stay wild
keep dancing free

as everything does
collapsing too soon
tonight
I am slow dancing
under the moon

KNIFE FIGHT

I was armed
with my heart and white flag
your hands held knives
aimed at both

- your aim was impeccable.

BUTTERFLY WOMAN

butterfly woman
crawl into yourself
and die

butterfly woman
spread your wings
and fly

butterfly woman
you are free
you are alive

butterfly woman
fly

BROKEN HOME

I left
my light on
door unlocked
fire roaring
warm meal waiting
fresh linen
tucked firmly
a place
to hang your jacket
weighted
by day's burdens
a pillow to rest
your head
my arms for shelter
I made myself
into a home for you

and your boots
only stood muddy
on the welcome mat

*- was it arson or an electrical issue
that caused me to burn up in flames?*

To War With Words

I do not want your sword
weakly held between both hands
lay it down, steady
I do not wish for a man

I have my own weapons
one firm in each hand
left, sharp and fire-bladed
right, dipped in poisonous brand

I am ready for war
with words, my power, my ink
and do not be mistaken, my dear
my pen is mightier
than you think

Don't Blame

don't close your eyes
and blame the stars for disappearing

don't cover your ears
and blame the birds for never singing

don't hold your breath
and blame the air for suffocating

don't stand still
and blame your legs for not moving

don't cage your heart
and blame love for never entering

don't pluck a rose
and blame it
for struggling
to bloom

SMALL TALK

save your small talk
for someone who cares
are there clouds, rain, or snow
up in the air
this is getting old
I don't care about the weather
but when it's cold
I still wear your sweater

ENDINGS

if I wrote you a novel
I wouldn't know where to start
beyond this lifetime
eons apart
but I remember the endings
a never-ending story
of tragedy
in the dark

and then

a spark

YOUR FLOWER

I was your flower
but you trampled carelessly over me
and dug me from the earth
ripping off my remaining petals
one
by
one
then you told me
to bloom

MY FLOWER

my seeds took root
in healthier soil
I rose from the dirt
and bloomed for myself
more radiant than ever
untouched
and in peace

BAIT AND SWITCH

a game of trickery once again
drawn into your trap to say the least
you had other plans for me
my hurricane heart desired peace

baited with sinister flattery
another hook to catch your prize
fingers crossed behind your back
as you sang a fishing song of lies

swim ahead of you, always I see
I am not as foolish as your tongue
I bless my words while yours deceive
an empty hook sinks undone

I am a different freedom fish now
immune to your poisonous bait
realising this, I cannot be caught
rage turns your switch back to hate

as you watch your prize

s w i m   *away*

YOUR TOY

my heart is not a plaything
you picked from your toy box
or a yo-yo on a string
that you can push away
and pull back in
at your will

do not be surprised
if my string begins to fray
and I do not wind back up to you
like I did so easily
like you expected before

my string will break
you will have played with me
for the last time

ENVY

oh green giant
jealousy never
looked good on you
envy my prides
degrade and claim them too
green hypocrite of deceit
climb your stalk of thorns
retreat
let your insecurities
become worn
plant your seeds
in your garden
fresh water flow
find your own
green grass
to grow

MY DEMON

last night I woke up
silently screaming
I dreamt of a demon with claws
playing tug-of-war with my soul
it would not let me go
so I did
and I pulled myself away
from the nightmare

it didn't take me long to realise
the demon I had to let go of

was you

PLAY

I was not afraid of his demons
nor was I ashamed of mine
sometimes
when they came out to play
they got along
just fine

- until love became a game to him,
and he lost his prize.

DIVIDED

loving you
is both heaven and hell
and when I kissed you
I was prepared
to burn

Poet And The Scientist

"How is a flower of love still growing from our ashes?"
said the poet.

"Volcanic ash is actually the best for growing, it's rich with
minerals and nutrients from deep inside the earth."
said the scientist.

"Then volcanic ash we shall be."
she said.

"Every natural disaster also breeds creation."
he said.

"Even ours."
they said.

- the magic in our disasters.

CLIMB

if you ever feel small
remind yourself
that you can climb mountains
and standing at the peak
you will be taller
than the mountain itself

FLAGS OF RED

I ignored every red flag
and trust me
there were enough
to stake into the surface
of the moon
and claim it
as my own

Twisted

loving you from a distance
you said as you stalked me

haunting me

a painful, twisted truth
dipped in dark romance

taunting me

WE ARE POWERFUL

I am a woman
body tempestuous
my hips
are thunder
and lightning
I shelter my heart
the eye of my storm
name me goddess
one powerfully striking
every mark on my body
a life-carved path
forming alleys towards
my rising
I created life pure
by motherly strength
I fear no hurricane
colliding

- we are women. we are mothers. we are survivors.
we are POWERFUL.

PREDATOR

I will never be your prey
you will never sink your teeth
into me
deep enough
to pierce
my soul
again

Go

I will
burn every bridge
sever every tie
break every chain
fray every rope
snap every branch
loosen every knot
release every fear
escape every prison
run every distance
walk through every fire
brave every storm
swim every current

and I will go

to the ends of this earth

to free myself from the hell

that is you

ABYSSAL

do not open your soul
to the abyss of a man
who has none

he will devour yours
and come back for more

he is a black hole
with no beginning
and no end

do not gaze upon him

- I almost lost mine.

RED QUEEN

she will be known
as the woman
who tore bravery
from beast
and wore it
as the crown
upon her head

ferocious beauty
as the cloak
of all she is
dipped
in ravenous
red

- the beast was brave enough to pursue her,
and she bit back instead.

51

TIME WARP

walk me through your wonders
I want to taste the stars
beneath your skin
let me caress the universe
drink your darkest veiled sins
entangle your magic into mine
a dance of souls entwined
and lead me to the core
of existence
take me back in time

GIFTED

you were divinely gifted
from the moment you were created
a unique and powerful magic
voices of angels sang elated
when you opened your newborn eyes
for the very first time in my arms
stars fell dancing into their light
keeping you safe from harm

and I was divinely gifted
the universe in my own two hands
carrying the heartbeat of my own wishing star
body meeting cosmic demands
a gift of a lifetime truly
feminine beauty of a mother ecstatic
love eternal that transcends infinite
my daughter, you are pure magic

*"You're everything a mother should be,
I am so proud of you."*

*- My mother,
on the birth of my daughter.*

QUESTIONS

I fear the day
my daughter asks me
who is her father
what is a father
where is her father
when will she have a father
why she doesn't have a father
how could a father walk away

who
what
where
when
why
how
?

OBEY

he said I never
listened to him
though I heard
every word
clearly
spoken
and unsaid

what he meant was
I did not obey
or submit
when his demands
sought to cage me
instead

- I am not a prisoner of love.

WOLF WOMAN

she learned to embrace
parts of herself
she never knew existed
let them run free and wild
untamed and ravenous
wild wolves beneath her skin
howling to be let loose
insatiable hunger craving life
clawing towards her surface
grinning at the moonlight
dancing under the stars
she finally felt herself
she was
alive

Vows

if you believe actions
come before words
just remember
that the vows are said
before
the rings are placed

SURREAL

to feel everything
so deeply
is to awaken a sense
not physical
and to experience life
in another dimension
far beyond
this existence

WATER

I am water, with ocean skin
my depths are feared
and unknown within
my strong current will pull you under
and my waves will carry you to shore

awaken a storm around my seas
and you will see my mighty roar
as I reflect the moonlight on my edges
in the darkest and blackest of night

I will drown you beneath me
as you try to outwit and escape
for the weak and unworthy
cannot outswim
the deepest ocean
of fate

FIRE

water craves fire
and you were my flame
a raging inferno
screaming my name
you fed your fire
with everything in your path
swallowed love, swallowed hate
and you never looked back
until you began to burn into me
and it scared you to finally see
I was sanctuary for your chaos
and the peace to all of your rage
that simply, I could end it all
with only a gentle wave
you wanted more
it was never enough
the fire within you
had more good to snuff
I had no choice left but to say
enough is enough
and end it today
my water doused your fire
the smoke
was seen for miles
now all that remains
is our ashes left in piles

AIR

I am wind, strong and true
a bitter chill to kiss your face
as I wrap myself around you
seeking warmth's embrace

breathe me in, and set me free
for I will return as a gentle breeze
flowing freely between the leaves
and I will find you again

and I will remind you
that I am a necessity to life
know that I have never left you
my hurricane of light

you will hear my name
with every breath you take
and every chill through your bones
will make your heart ache
until you breathe
me in again

EARTH

I am forest
I am tree
deep are the roots
that grow beneath me
here I stand tall
within my sanctuary
come forth a companion
I have yearned
for eternity

look, stand
and wonder
feel the wisdom in my bark
let my branches come down
and bury you into the dark

we will grow together
withstand every storm
reach for the sunlight
our roots never to be torn

SPIRIT

I am not from this ordinary place
I belong elsewhere
dancing among the stars in space
I love, I feel, I see
with my mind, heart, and soul
far beyond the mere physical
a transcendent touch
a goddess of love
a flame in search of a twin
sent by the forces above

everything is connected
like 1, 4, and 3
awaken and find me somewhere
in our dreams

speak without words
and I will understand
touch me without touching
without the use of our hands
see without looking
eyes closed and believing
another lifetime awaits
and I will be waiting

TRANSCENDENT

I loved you
beyond our bodies
past our vision
beyond our fingertips
on flesh

god damn
I loved you

with my soul

with yours

WRITE

I said I would write
about you
about us
about me
about love
I am keeping my promise

TWISTED FATE

the universe is with us
but my darling
this lifetime
is not

WHITE LIGHT

blood of the mother
parts of us two
braided strands of fate
purple, red, and blue

bring peace to our angel
connect us to you

divinely created
in love
are you

MY TEMPLE

my body is an ornate temple
and should be treated as such
magic within these walls of flesh
can be revealed with sacred touch

if you gaze upon my eyes
an ancient soul lies within
a rainbow full of mysteries
a story of love and sin

though some walls may crumble
from past lives and memories old
I am still standing, gleaming
a beacon for futures untold

my body is a temple
where light and dark reside
be cautious where you tread upon
a goddess lives inside

TONIGHT I CRIED

Tonight, I cried as I rocked my sweet baby girl to sleep.

It was one of those moments that are gone too soon, that you wish you could freeze and keep forever.

As I held her, I sang to her the song I have always sung to her since she came into this world, "you are my sunshine, my only sunshine…" and I rocked her gently and peacefully as she drifted off to sleep, curled up at my breast surrounded by my safe and loving arms. Our nightly routine.

Tonight, I cried because I saw myself in her at that moment, like looking into a mirror of innocence. As the memories of my entire life passed through my mind, the good and the bad, I am looking at and holding this brand new, beautiful life that I have created, and I cried because this is just the beginning.

Tonight, I cried because I realised that a mother's hopes and dreams for her child are even bigger than her own, and fuelling their potential with love is everything.

Tonight, I cried because I know and feel the strength of our bond and unconditional love we share as mother and daughter.

Tonight, I cried because I held my entire heart and soul in my arms, protecting her for eternity.

Tonight, I cried because there is no better feeling in the world than being a mother, and when I look at her and hold her, I am filled with love and I know my life has meaning.

There is nothing more perfect, natural, and rewarding than this.

1 YEAR

12 months
52 weeks
365 days
8, 765 hours
525, 948 minutes
31, 556, 926 seconds

1 year ago you came into this world and changed my life forever. It was a new life for both of us. My heart now lives outside my body.

12 months ago I held you in my arms and kissed your beautiful face for the first time, and I cried so many happy tears each time you looked into my eyes.

52 weeks ago you fell asleep in my arms so peacefully and you have every night since, knowing that I would never leave you and keep you safe always.

365 days I have woken up to your smiling face and big blue eyes and I have fallen asleep with you curled up next to me, your hand almost always over my heart.

8, 765 hours we have shared together learning, playing, laughing, singing, dancing, reading, crying, sleeping, eating, nursing, bonding, and so much more.

525, 948 minutes filled with hopes and dreams for you and wishes for your future, you are always the first thought in my mind and my heart. You always come first.

31, 556, 926 precious seconds that you have known love, safety, happiness, trust, comfort, and protection. Knowing that no matter what, your mama will always be here for you, and you will always be my beautiful baby.

My Star

once upon a lifetime
I wished on a star
opened my dreaming eyes
my soul whispered
there you are

- my twinkle little star, E. ☆

I Know You

love
recognition
at first sight

- hello again.

CHRISTMAS MAGIC

I know that Christmas
will be hard for us both
so let this remind you
to hold onto your glimmer of hope
despite everything
we've said and done
in our senseless war
never to be won
believing and saying things
we both know aren't true
despite all of this, I forgive you
I wanted to make you an ornament
that reminds me of another galaxy
or a bright starry night
if you look at it
in just the right light
with a little Christmas sparkle
a hint of magic too
some wishing stars
pulled from the sky
and just a dash of
purple, red, and blue

- 2017

BECOMING

if you hold hate
you become anger
if you hold resentment
you become guilt
if you hold onto bad
you will ignore and forget the good
if you hold lies
you will never be truth
if you keep yourself in the dark
you will never be light

and the most frustrating part is
I couldn't save you from yourself

I was pouring my light into you
but your darkness
was only a black hole

MUTE

I stopped speaking your name
when I finally realised
it didn't deserve the sound of my voice
or the breath in my lungs
that quick flutter of my heart
as it slides from my tongue
or the crack in my throat
as I ~~choke~~
on the memories
that come up with it

I stopped speaking your name
because it gave you more life
while siphoning mine still
as it left my body
with every syllable

HUNGRY AS A WOLF

how can a monster
with no soul
regret creating magic
within a woman
who carried more soul
within her
than her own

- he ate them both,
and demanded thirds.

HE SAID, SHE SAID

he said
it was a man's right
for a woman to carry his child
whether she likes it, or not

he said
all women are selfish, disgusting
whores, sluts, bitches, hoes

he said
marriage is only
blue balls, loneliness, disappointment
when he didn't receive
what he demanded

he said
I can say whatever I want
do whatever I want
and you will not leave
or I will find you
because you are mine

he said
a good woman stays
within her prison
for her man
or else she does not love him
and never did

he said
go and die
I don't care

she said
no

and she was the monster

*- he spoke about his mother, daughter, sisters,
and every woman with his words.*

FOREVER

tonight I dreamt that we flew
to another world
far from this one
and the moon was so close to us
our eyes filled with magic
and hope upon looking at it
it was so close
we could hold it in our hands
feel stars on our skin
and taste forever on the surface
before we flew away
and woke up

- I'll love you in my dreams
because there, we are infinite.

1:43am

WILDFIRES

it's wildfire season
where I met you
stronger than last year
when I left you

perhaps it's the change in the wind
creeping her flames towards you
hotter and brighter
roaring with revenge
slowly seeking you out

she will lick the icy peaks
across the mountaintops
until she devours what she seeks
Karma, in her dress of furious flames
will swallow you and choke you
in what you deserve
what you gave me

your own taste
of hell

Fire And Water

if, by chance
the universe has spoken
will we both listen
should her spell be broken
a call to each soul
in love, bound yet broken
reseal our fate for us both
we have chosen

douse the flames of Karma
let her hear; all is forgiven
a lesson to be learned
we received and are living

divinely united
our souls will not part
let water calm fire
rage is only love
in our hearts

F WORDS

fear and forgiveness
fight like lovers do
fear of everything going
fear of everything returning

though forgiveness and peace
is not just for them
nor is it
another chance

it is for your growing wings
it is for your freedom dance
it is for your healing heart
it is for you refusing to burn
down into their flames
any longer

that, they should fear
forgiveness
makes you stronger

- I forgive the unforgiveable,
and set us both free.

DEMONS TO ANGELS

she had a forceful ambition
that raised demons from pyre
vengeful twister of fate
a resurrection from hellfire

she had the ferocity of a whip
to tear angels from space
decorated their wings
a retribution from grace

she had the power of a queen
sinners crave delicious mercy
smiled as they lust for her
begging, pleading, thirsty

she turned hell into heaven
order restored, chaos seized
angels and demons fell to their knees
as searing kisses whispered to her
save me, goddess
please

- she saved herself instead.

CREATING MAGIC

I told myself
that my words could create life
so I placed my hands upon the pages
and felt my heart beating
the rise and fall of my chest

I told myself
my words could devastate cities
but I would much rather
bury them in love
instead

I told myself
that my words could create magic
with only the stroke of my pen
so I closed my eyes
and scribbled blindly
I wrote
about you
until the end

- abracadabra.

SPEAK TO THE DEVIL

I'm not sure why I still write about you
it's unlikely these words are read
some twisted dark part of me
still hopes you glimpse of red

though often I must remind myself
you ignored three words so well
how could I possibly expect
a thousand more to reach your hell

- if the Devil could receive letter mail.

My Storm

try to steal
my thunder
you're bound
to be struck
by my lightning
this is my storm
not yours
and I am dancing up
something
frightening

- watch your step.

WRITER'S WOES

writers grieve differently
instead of our faces held in hands
we hold blank pages
open and ready
tears that fall are not tears at all
but are words carefully placed
heavy

- we bleed in ink.

TRINITY

I stood before him
vulnerable and willing
stripped beyond my flesh
he gazed upon not just me
revealing
mind
body
soul
as I fell to my knees
we awakened the binds
of our tragic trinity

- sacred memories.

FAIRY TALES

little girls are taught
to
twirl and sparkle
dance free as air
pluck daisies into bouquets
bejewel braided hair
wait
silently with smiles
pretty wondrous eyes
dresses fit for princesses
a pleasant disguise
for
magic wishes sent by fairies
towered hearts by dragon's guard
damsel's distress carried
be graceful, though it's hard
his
fairy tale princely armour
a dreamy kiss to awaken
rare love once upon a rhyme
patiently saved, then taken
rescue
yourself this time

PIVOTAL

if you told me to choose
a pivotal moment in my life
I could choose from many

my birth
my first heartbreak
my daughter's birth
my 100th heartbreak

life entirely is a pivotal moment
the process of changing, healing
learning, growing, aging
makes us into who we are

the only true pivotal experience
within life itself
is time
and time, like life
is *infinite*

SINNERS

tell me that I am going to hell
I will laugh, and smile
I have already been there
I have danced with the devil
until I myself was a raging inferno
I have tasted, consumed hell
a delicious sin
we called love

hell
is
home

SLITHER

we are
immortal souls
all snakes
my love
trapped within
mortal bodies
until the next life
sheds our skin
we slither and coil
together

MADNESS

in order to view life
from outside of life
one must first dip their toes
into the murky waters of madness
open eyes, empty lungs
dive in
and emerge

- I hope you know how to swim.

OPEN BOOK

I was told I should share
my writing with the world
but to do so would mean opening up
my book, my soul, my heart, my life
to tear down my own walls
I spent my entire life building
and leaving myself vulnerable
for all to judge, love, hate

how do you share your story
to even those who would rather
see your pages burn

- I might just be crazy enough to do it.

HOPE

all my life I have lived silently with
depression, anxiety, bipolar, PTSD
and I say lived, not struggled
because these illnesses
have been a blessing in disguise
I have been able to feel deeper
see deeper, and experience reality
with a different set of eyes
to see a broad spectrum
of the colors of life
to value the good and the beautiful
the evil and the darkness
I have pulled myself out
of the darkest of black holes
and came out shining brighter
than the stars
I do not fear solidarity
loneliness, or even death
instead I embrace it
and find solace
inside every experience
life has to offer
because in every corner
of my dark mind
there is hope

ASCENDING

in a divine union
if one soul ascends before the other
rather than together as one
a massive shift in communication
and connection will occur
causing a rift between the two
and a constant struggle
to restore their balance
one ascends, the other falls
you fell, and I rose higher
I am out of your reach in this state
in this frequency of existence
and I will not lower myself
because you refused
to rise with me
into a purple-hazed realm
of nirvana

- match my soul. match my energy.
- it's beautiful here.

EMBERS

do not be surprised
if I don't warm up
to the same fire that burned me
trust, like love
can also go up in flames
and my ashes
are still
smouldering

WITCH

you tried to burn me
set my soul on fire with hate
scorch me and lick me
with your flames

darling, you failed

this is a witch
you cannot burn

LADY OF WATER

calm as the sea
moods like the tides
strength of the waves
rain from her eyes
goddess of water
ruler of torrent
lured to depths
by siren's lament

FULL MOON

there's something poetically tragic
about staring out
of my bedroom window alone

watching the full moon rising
patiently awaiting her return
a graceful grand entrance
floating above the trees
an angel's halo approaches
reminding me of the beauty
in the darkness

and she shines
her full luminous light
upon me and I am recharged
I am one with the moon
in this moment
and always

SCARED

it's bad again
thoughts are being jumbled
speech is but a mumble
I am trying to remain humble
but inside I am afraid

I am frantic, panicking, unravelling
days are merging into weeks
time is rushing too fast
it's this place, it must be
a prison inside my mind
except now the bars are my arms
and the walls are ivy that bind

I rarely ever sleep
and tears come fast, can never last
I am ashamed to revert to this state
in secret, and in hiding
instead of strong, I now feel weak
always held onto you
leading me through the dark
onwards up to the peak

soon I will have to let go
of your hand, you
the only thing that makes me whole
my heart outside my body

out of sight although
never out of mind
I gave you life
but you saved mine
my daughter
I promise you
I will always find
until the end of time

- I am not losing you. I am not losing you.
I am not losing you.

- am I losing me?

- a mother's fears as her child grows older.

I Survived You

you will attempt to dirty my name
but it will never be as dirty
as your hands and your mouth
or as muddy, and murky
as your past, your present
your entire existence

your sweet nothings
are neither sweet
nor are they something
to believe in foolishly
like a child devouring
a twisted poisonous treat

your vengeance is not truth
your insecurities and hate
are rooted not in your chains on me
but in your abyssal youth
your first date

I will never be a quiet woman
to sit down, shut up, be silenced
I will rise from the ashes
of the fire you burned me in

and this bird of flames
will wear the name, Karma; flying

you have blood on your hands
and dirt in your fingertips
from the grave you dug for yourself
smiled, licked your lips
pillows of rocks, blankets of worms
splinters from the casket
made of your thorns

you will rest in your hell
consumed by your hate
swallowed in your darkness
behold your fate
alone, as you deserve
as you wished, you have been served

so lay yourself quietly down
and count very slowly
the nightmares of your destruction
weaved into your invisible crown
lonely

- hell hath no fury like a dragon reborn.

Army

surround yourself with good people
who love you and care for you
and you will assemble
an army of light and love
to stand beside you
against the darkness
to carry you through any storm
you never have to fight alone
for in love and light
you were born

WATER BECOMES FIRE

and so water became fire
in the clenched fist of hate
no longer slipping through fingers
she bit back and gave him
a hot burning taste

ONE

I have ONE goddamn lifetime
in this body, this world, this skin
ONE lifetime of memories
until the next one begins
I'll be damned if I give the devil
the satisfaction of watching it burn
to lay waste to my paradise
forced into silence, wait my turn
there is no way in hell
I am allowing a soulless demon
destroy any chance of happiness
I bring into my life, I am screaming!

god damnit I am living it to the end
and I am free
not a second more I will waste
no more
into he

RAINBOW EYES

rainbow eyes
you have galaxies in your soul
a spectrum of color
prisms within your bones
simply one shade of the cosmos
cannot be enough to behold
only those worthy of you may
plunge into your universe
the stars as a whole
bathing in the supernova
your rainbow eyes unfold
rainbow eyes
cosmic jewels
stories
untold

SELENE VIOLET

red and blue
made purple with love
her violet wings
flew out of reach above

a beautiful masterpiece
once in this lifetime
we could not hold in our arms
still once you were mine

never the same
we blended for hours
that shade of purple
should have been ours

howling at the moon
red and blue together
our calls were answered
the magic in your feathers

we named you
Selene Violet
our angel
forever

I Am Goddess

darling, did you really believe
that you calling me a goddess
made it so
as if rescinding your flattery
would strip me of my title
the moment I said; no
as if I didn't already know what I was
before you recognized it in me
claimed ownership of my power
as if you gave me
who I was for free
as if it were up to you
to place this crown upon my head
my wings are forged in fire
there is nothing that I dread
I made myself before you
and I will rise higher since
I have been her all my life
for this I need not convince
believe me when I tell you this
my strength did not come cheap

you will soon realise
a goddess
is not made
for the weak

RED AND BLUE

she was red
a flaming goddess
of equal love and rage
not afraid of passion
or her devilish gaze
a bloody hellfire
the angel of sin
that lived and loved
the fire within

he was blue
with depths unknown
a calm ocean true
yet a secret he held to hide
a torrent in himself too
hurricanes are calm
before they begin
behold his destruction
the storm within

THEIR STORM

together they made purple
in the skies as storms clash
eventually water will drown fire
until all that remains is ash

the smoke that will rise
from their merciless days
will fill the air in a violet haze

and the storms
laid themselves
to rest

Revenge

it will never be revenge
in my heart that I seek
hate is but an emotion
loved only by the weak

- I want peace.

BLACK HOLES

people can be black holes too
vortexes of negative energy
a black abyss at their heart
suffocators of any flicker of light
even a tiny spark
you can feel their claws pulling at you
as if your arms, legs, and body become
stretched, torn, manipulated
drawn inescapably into them
and they do take you to another place
though not as magical as you would imagine
no flashing lights, star-kissed fingers
where your skin should tingle but instead
it sears like flaming pins beneath the surface
being repeatedly struck by lightning, falling
into their downward spiral
no light, no rescue, only
an inverted tunnel of razor teeth
that will shred you apart
if you try to escape

people can be black holes too
I have the scars to prove it

ABANDONED

I vividly remember
a long hallway, an open door
standing frozen, confused
bare feet on cold basement floor

a heavy door that slammed shut
and took you away with it
watching with childhood eyes
abandoned reality hit

I hoped you would
come back, you might
but my father
did not
kiss me goodnight

SPEAK

if you think my voice is loud
you should hear the *s c r e a m s*
within my silent words

DAYDREAMERS

men will dream
of owning a powerful woman

until they realise
her strength is larger
than their hands can hold
her voice is louder
than their roar can bellow
her blood boils
their veins so icy cold
her height measures higher
than their fragile ego

and they will try to make her small
break her down to their level

but little do they know
she is rising still

HOME

you and I
will always be
unfinished business
no matter how many times
I turn my pages
end my chapters
close my books
try to erase you
remove your hooks
you were a part of me
brutally carved in stone
the pain of your love
sometimes
brings me home

- a.k.a. Stockholm syndrome?

RIFT

I hope you can forgive me
as I forgave too
I froze in my space broken
unable to save you
I had to do
what needed to be done
neither of us in this war
have won

it had to end somehow
your vengeance is over
now take a bow
prison bars are colder

damage can be healed
and words replaced
I am sorry for the pain
we have dealt, ego's race
and in our beating hearts
hate took love's place

now nothing we felt
can save us from this
jagged rift between us
dark twisted bliss

PURGATORY

neither heaven nor hell
may have wanted you
but how lucky you were
for I was a bit of both
purgatory
in the cosmos

To The Grave

will you bury me
into the dirt with you
we dug our graves
why not share them too
flesh on flesh
cold air breathed in
darkest nights
crave blessed sins
run my fingertips
through the earth with yours
plant seeds of life
love's rebirth, nature's course
howl together at the moon
one last time
your soul collided
once with mine

SMILE

when you struggle to find your smile
I hope you remember mine
be still, reminisce for a while
thank the stars for good and bad
the beautiful taste of madness
that we had
look at the moon
I look at it too
smile for me
I'll smile for you

SUNFLOWERS

my grandmother
grew tall sunflowers
strong and vibrant
like her
she has been gone
for long years past
though she is everywhere
I turn
I always
followed sunflowers
to guide me, not lose sight
along flowered paths
reminding me
to keep hold of my light
but I am confused
in the winter
when I no longer
see them in bloom
then I remember
sunflowers
reaching for the sun
and so will I
soon

WAR PAINT

I told you I wore makeup
for myself
to make me feel pretty
though I already knew I was
without it

you told me I wore makeup
for someone else
to make me feel pretty
though they already knew I was
without it

and we both lied

it's my war paint
when confident
it's my excuse not to cry
when weak

- though black stained tears are pretty, too.

SEASONS

feeling the seasons change in the air
always sets me in a panic
change is good though I still fear
experiencing it without you
the first leaves turning red
that crunch beneath our feet
crisp air into our lungs
and candy apple treats
summer flowers blooming
and butterfly kisses
spring puddle jumping
thunderstorm wishes
hot chocolate and marshmallows
as a cold winter will freeze
white snowflakes on our tongues
sparkling ornaments on the tree
fireworks for a new year
new beginnings do come
seasons change all the time
still we stayed young

and I wanted every moment
every season
everything
with you

HUSH

hush now my love
close your tired eyes
lay yourself to rest
a magical world
is waiting for you
place your head
upon my chest
hush now my darling
tomorrow is a new day
a dreamland's bridge
brings future's reality
stars will dance and sway
hush now my baby
I am with you
hold my hand and sleep
smile as the moon
sings you a song
and the lullaby
you will forever keep
hush now my love
drift off to sleep
today is over
a new will begin
dream with magic in your eyes
the rainbows you hold within

COSMIC LOVERS

share your universe with me
bead the stars around my neck
arrange the planets a path to love
tease me astronomically, at best
I want to taste the aura of purple
with every lick of your tongue
pull me into the orbit of you
eyes eclipse as we become one
a supernova of ascension
colored explosions in plain sight
while I ride you into the milky way
my cosmic armoured knight

- our stars are bright tonight.

A Monster Named Blue

the monsters I still live with
are not beneath my restless bed
or in the darkness of my closet
they are memories inside my head

beasts hiding in the corners
of my mind
woven demons into the fabric
of my soul
shadows lurking through the corridors
of my heart

and once upon a time
I fell in love with one of them
he used to have a name, too
and if I have to speak it
silently
I will simply name him
Blue

GHOST

try to forget me

I
dare
you

you will feel me everywhere

I
will
haunt
you

REST

keep going
keep fighting
keep living
keep breathing
keep standing
keep loving
keep yourself alive

but when do I
rest

ICE CREAM

a scoop of stress
on top of anxiety
on top of depression
on top of physical pain
on top of mental exhaustion
on top of insomnia
on top of emotional trauma
sprinkled with abuse
is like an ice cream cone
with too many scoops on it
before it falls down
and hits the ground
melting
until it's washed away
and the colors

        r
         u
          n
            o
            u
           t

GOODBYE

I don't know how you sleep at night
the nightmares keep me awake
shield my eyes from dreaming of you
burning me at the stake

I survived you and I'm still breathing
though each breath burns in my lungs
I wish I could stand tall with pride
and marvel at how far I've come

but every day feels like I'm hiking
up a mountain with no peak in sight
I will have to live with this pain
for the rest of my cherished life

I hope you are proud of yourself
you'll forget me and I'll try too
but for now my heart is bleeding red
to eliminate every trace of your blue

FEATHERS

a thousand feathers could fall
and I would collect them all
floating hope among heaven's call
a reminder that I am not alone

each feather, one for my wings
to rise and fly away
wind to lift me up above
challenges will never stay

thank you for these feathers
storm clouds always clear
angels all around me

I hope
peace is near

MOTHER KNOWS BEST

my mother taught me many lessons
my best friend through it all
the strongest woman that I know
she would rise with every fall
she carried the weight of the world
on only her two shoulders
something I could not understand
until I myself grew older
a mother of my own daughter now
I follow closely in her footsteps
overcoming all of the worst
and still hoping for the best
I wish that I had listened closer
before I closed my childhood door
spent more time in her arms at rest
I suppose I had to learn for myself
mother knows best
and more

- I love you mom, you were right.

ABSENT

the men in my life
never tried to be permanent figures
perhaps that's how I learned
to recognize the difference between
what I needed
what I deserved
and most certainly
what I did not

WAR

take up your sword, my darling
steady your crown upon your head
there are dragons to slay in darkness
feared queen of merciless red

light that emerges in the shadows
will not be that of beast
but flames of her beauty ignited
a raging war to reclaim her peace

- *there are more monsters to defeat.*

WAKE ME UP

tell me that I'm not in love with him
that I'm still asleep in a dream
tell me that this is a nightmare
awaken me, I'll silence a scream
tell me none of this is real
and I will let out a sigh
relieve me from the chains of him
a caged bird
is desperate to fly

MEDUSA

if our paths should cross again
my gaze will turn your heart to stone
a gift for you to experience
the remainder of this lifetime alone

and if by chance you've realised
the damage you have done
I hope you let out a frozen shriek
that will be heard by no one

I'll find your statue in the next
though lifeless you will remain
until your stone-cold lips are kissed
with a kiss no longer in vain

and only I
can wake
you up

ROSES

he gave me roses
thorns were skin deep
he gave me roses
hid the monster beneath
he gave me roses
red true as heart's swell
he gave me roses
never dried tears fell
he gave me roses
I kept every one
he gave me roses
dark chains now come
he gave me roses
kissed me in vain
he gave me roses
branded his pain
he gave me roses
for promises do not keep

but he gave me roses
so
he must love me

DREAMING IN PURPLE

dreaming in purple
swimming
in the shades of my soul divine
beauty in the color I love
brings me peace as a whole combined

an equal balance of red and blue
a perfect purple I can do
I have both colors inside of me
brighter and truer too

my life is much like a rainbow
every color has a story, a rhyme
reaching for the stars in me
shades in between
forever frozen in time

but purple, my love, purple
purple
will always be mine

BREADCRUMBS

messages from the universe
we hold in our hands
observed with our eyes
magic withstands
a number
143
color
purple
memory
quantum entangled
we

serendipitous coincidence
synchronic instances
carried by thread
across any distance
that leads me
back
to you

collect each breadcrumb
for they last for a moment
remember the message
before reality returns

a path to the stars
I'll find your arms there
floating in space
reaching
through magic
in the air

where nothing else matters
just us two

my red
your blue

everything happens
for a reason

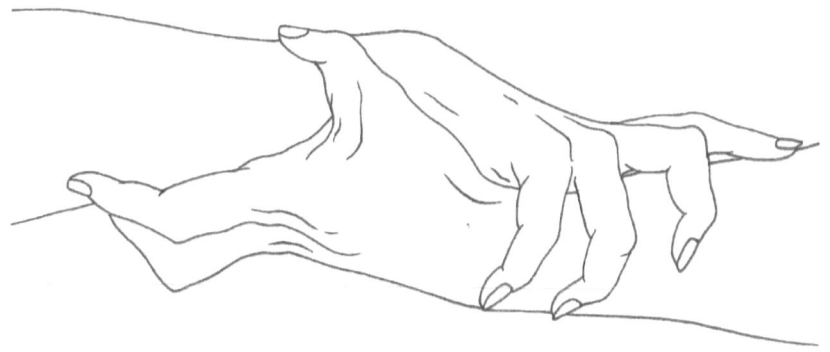

DREAMING
IN
PURPLE

all my
love
Thank
you

143

A Letter To My Daughter

The world today is cruel, unfair, unjust, and relentless. People are fighting against people, hate has become more prominent than love, and tragedy after tragedy unfolds daily.

You won't understand what is happening in the world but one day you will, and I hope you know that love will always win.

Be cautious and careful, some people are wolves in sheep's clothing and cannot be trusted. Trust in yourself and your intuition – it will almost always be right.

Stand up for yourself and show kindness, be the strength when others have none. Protect yourself and those you love, because tomorrow is never promised. Spend your time wisely, do not take it for granted. Live your life to the fullest and be happy, successful, and surrounded by love.

You are beautiful and unique, don't let anyone ever tell you different or make you feel like you are less than amazing.

You are strong and fierce. You matter. You are important. You are divinely loved, no matter what you do in life or where you go, or who you become. You are so loved.

When life gets hard and the world around you is falling at your feet, stand strong and don't crumble with it. Find your strength and don't give up. Always move forward. Believe in yourself.

You will find your path and I will be with you every step of the way, and to catch you when you fall. Remember, everything happens for a reason.

yes, my darling
the dirt is dark
rooted
with the past
but look
my darling
at the beauty
and new life
that grows
and blooms
from it

When you feel like the darkest dirt, close your eyes, and imagine the flowers growing from the deepest parts of you. Feel their colours. You know what waters them?
Love. Hope. *You.*

Love, Mama ♥
xoxoxo
P.S. Don't be afraid
to breathe some
fire. L 18

THE IMPORTANCE OF WORDS

Some may say actions are more important, but to me, words are everything. The foundation.

Words are not temporary. They can create, break, promise, destroy. Words are our raw thoughts and emotions brought into reality by voice, pen, and ink.

Some may use words to deceive, lie, manipulate, destroy, and coerce. This is not their purpose. There is wisdom behind the saying, "think before you speak" and "choose your words wisely" because words have the power to damage as much as they do to repair.

I will always appreciate the words that come before the actions, because when we speak it comes from a place inside our souls that reveals the truth about us before the actions take place.

Words are everything to me, and how you choose to use them, relate to them, interpret, or understand them is left to you, the reader. Sometimes, the only place I can feel and love freely is in my writing.

So I observe, think, write, read, listen, and turn tragedy into poetry, life into lesson, because the mind can be a beautiful hell to live in.

words left unsaid
may be forgotten
in your head
but written
they will live forever

Special Thanks

My daughter, who taught me that there is always a reason to smile, something to fight for, and everything to hope for. You reminded me to slow down and live in every moment, and showed me the true meaning of unconditional love. You are my rock and my power to keep going. You are my sunshine when skies are grey. I love you to the moon and beyond. You always come first.

My mother, who passed down her strength and always believed in me. She gave me wings large enough to fly on my own so I could learn the challenges and lessons of life, good and bad, and how to overcome them with grace and beauty. You are my best friend.

My brother, who has survived a great deal of his darkness and is still fighting monsters of his own. I hope you know that your family will always be here for you and there is nothing you can't overcome. I believe in you. Thank you for believing in me, and pushing me to finish my first book and continue writing.

My father, computer genius and lifetime tech-nerd, who always told me to pursue my passions and artistic talents. I will make you proud, I promise. My grandmother who loved her children, grandchildren, and nourished the lives of others as well as her own garden. I wish we had more time together and I know that you are always with me. I will never forget you and our memories together. I love you and I miss you always, until we meet again.

My friends and family, who no matter how far across time or distance have always supported me through my successes, failures, hopes, dreams, and messy healing throughout my life. Thank you for caring. You're my army of light.

My grandfather, who lived a long life of memories, love, and exploration around the world. Thank you for sharing your wisdom and history of your life and our family with me. I will cherish everything forever and continue to write as you and your father did as well. I am hopeful for generations to come. You are missed greatly – "love you bunches" & hugs.

To the ones who have loved me and shared parts of their souls with me, for in every ending there is a beginning and every experience is a lesson. I hope you have a life of peace and happiness. I wish you well.

And lastly, thank you to the man who loved me and destroyed me while holding the entirety of my soul in his hands. You showed me that love is more than a word, and touch is more than a body. You taught me that I am so much more than a woman and brought forth the power I had in me all along. I will not suffer in the shadow of your destruction as you hoped, but instead I will rise and turn my pain into beauty, my stars into supernovas. I hope Karma wraps herself gently around you, kisses you mercilessly, and stays a companion for life. My love for you will transcend even this lifetime and inspire me for eons to come. Until the next, 143.

About The Writer

Leanna Hewitt (LUNAIRIS) was born and raised in Ontario, Canada and fell in love with literature and poetry at a young age, influenced by writers such as William Shakespeare, Friedrich Nietzsche, Robert Frost, Edgar Allan Poe, and Stephen King, she often spent her time alone with a book in her hands.

Expressing herself using her artistic and creative talents became a way of living and coping while overcoming obstacles in her life and in her mind.

She is a lover of all things romantic, astronomical, cosmic, magical, fantasy, and unknown. Her creativity thrives in the wake of chaotic lows and ecstatic highs.

Becoming a single mother with a daughter at the age of 22 and living in a small town nestled in the northern mountains of British Columbia for some time, she gained a wealth of wisdom, strength, and inspiration as love blossomed and also withered. Since returning to Ontario, she has been actively persuing her passion in becoming a writer and sharing her story with the world.

Coping with loss, battling mental illness, and healing from a tragic romance while remaining strong for her daughter is reflected through her writing.

She strives to turn her pain into power and appreciate the beauty that life has to offer, ultimately breaking the chains that held her in the past and learning to pull herself from the darkness. She hopes to light a beacon of hope for women and mothers who are struggling to escape abusive relationships.

DREAMING IN PURPLE is her first collection of writing and poetry. She is in the process of writing her next book and looks forward to sharing it with the world.

Her pen name, *LUNAIRIS*, is a tribute to the moon (luna) and Greek Goddess Iris, Goddess of the rainbow and messenger to the Olympian Gods. She describes her life as a rainbow ruling over events and emotions within every color, while delivering messages to her readers between heaven and earth, much like Iris used the rainbow as a bridge between the land and sky.

In Loving Memory

Richard Edgar H.
lifetime explorer and grandfather

June 11, 1937 – October 28, 2018

may you travel many lightyears, galaxies away
take more photos, I would love to see them one day

Selene Violet
pure soul with wings of an angel

January 18, 2017

sleep and rest peacefully your beautiful eyes
may our angels guide you safely into paradise

Michael Richard H.
mentor and beloved father

October 24, 1959 – August 9, 2015

I hope you find your starship in the sky
my footsteps are following you here closeby

Ana P.
cherished loving grandmother (baba)

September 6, 1943 – August 23, 2008

may your sunflowers shine tall and gardens grow
holding all angel children safe and close

always in my heart, until we meet again

DREAMING
IN
PURPLE